THE PERSON BEHIND THE BRAND

Henry Ford

Written by Annette Whipple

Illustrated by Gary Boller

TABLE OF CONTENTS

A Starfish Book

SEAHORSE PUBLISHING

Teaching Tips for Caregivers:

As a caregiver, you can help your child succeed in school by giving them a strong foundation in language and literacy skills and a desire to learn to read.

This book helps children grow by letting them practice reading skills.

Reading for pleasure and interest will help your child develop reading skills and will give your child the opportunity to practice these skills in meaningful ways.

- Encourage your child to read on their own at home.
- Encourage your child to practice reading aloud.
- Encourage activities that require reading.
- Establish a reading time.
- Talk with your child.
- Give your child writing materials.

Teaching Tips for Teachers:

Research shows that one of the best ways for students to learn a new topic is to read about it.

Before Reading

- Read the "Words to Know" and discuss the meaning of each word.
- Read the back cover to see what the book is about.

During Reading

- When a student gets to a word that is unknown, ask them to look at the rest of the sentence to find clues to help with the meaning of the unknown word.
- Ask the student to write down any pages of the book that were confusing to them.

After Reading

- Discuss the main idea of the book.
- Ask students to give one detail that they learned from the book by showing a text-dependent answer from the book.

Henry Ford—
Ford Motor Company

Henry Ford did not invent the car.

He became famous for making cars.

Henry Ford was born in 1863.

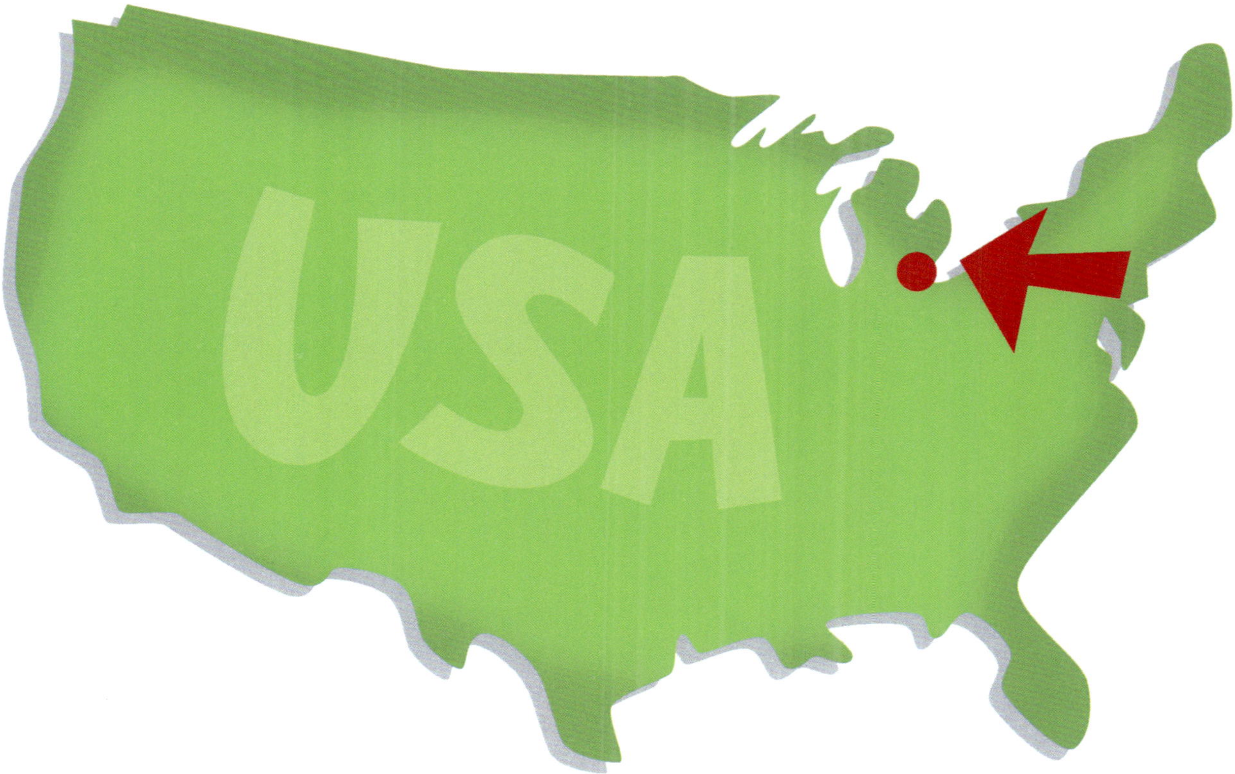

He grew up near Detroit, Michigan.

Henry was a **curious** boy.

He learned by doing.

Henry tied a lid to a pot over a fire.

The water burned Henry.

He learned to be more careful.

Young Henry had a watch.

He took it apart.

He learned how it worked.

Soon, Henry fixed watches for others.

He made his own tools from nails and knitting needles.

Henry learned about early cars.

He built one at home.

Henry wanted to make cars with better **engines**.

He made more cars.

Sometimes he failed, but he always learned a lot.

VAROOM

Henry created two car companies that did not last long.

Then, he started the Ford
Motor Company.

It is still going.

Henry built his **factory** with an **assembly line**.

A big, moving **belt** moved cars from worker to worker.

Each worker added one part.

Factories still use assembly lines like Henry's.

Cars built on an assembly line cost less.

More people could buy them.

Henry built a car called the Model T.

It was a big success!

We remember Henry Ford.

He was an **innovator**.

Henry Ford in 1919

He started with other people's ideas.

He made them better.

Words to Know

assembly line (uh-SEM-blee line): an arrangement in a factory in which a product passes from one person or machine to the next with each performing one small task until the product is complete

belt (belt): a continuous band of rubber used for moving things along a line

curious (KYOOR-ee-uhs): eager to know or learn about something

engines (EN-jinz): machines that provide the energy to make something move; machines under the hood of a car that take in gasoline or other fuels and supply the power to make the car go

factory (FAK-tur-ee): a building where products such as cars are made in large numbers

innovator (IN-uh-vay-tur): someone who has a talent for thinking of new ideas or new ways of doing things

Index

Comprehension Questions

1. As a boy, Henry Ford liked to ______ .

a. play baseball

b. learn new things

c. swim

2. On __________ , a belt moves cars from worker to worker.

a. a Model T

b. an engine

c. an assembly line

3. True or false: Henry learned how to fix other people's watches.

4. True or false: Henry made some of his own tools.

5. True or false: Henry always got it right the first time.

Answers:
1. b, 2. c, 3. True, 4. True, 5. False

About the Author

Annette Whipple celebrates curiosity through her books. She wrote *The Laura Ingalls Wilder Companion*, *Whooo Knew? The Truth About Owls*, and *Quirky Critter Devotions*. She lives with her family in Pennsylvania where she appreciates the natural beauty around her. Get to know Annette at www.AnnetteWhipple.com.

About the Illustrator

Gary Boller lives in the glorious countryside in Hampshire, UK, with his wife and two children, one Chihuahua, and four cats. He always doodled as a kid, even on his parents' walls, and loved the comics of the day. Gary also loves music and has played double bass in bands. He has toured all over Europe many times and the USA twice. He's currently learning fiddle, much to the annoyance of his pets.

Written by: Annette Whipple
Illustrated by: Gary Boller
Designed by: Under the Oaks
Editor: Kim Thompson

Library of Congress PCN Data
Henry Ford / Annette Whipple
The Person Behind the Brand
ISBN 979-8-8945-9116-2 (hard cover)
ISBN 979-8-8945-9121-6 (paperback)
ISBN 979-8-8945-9131-5 (EPUB)
ISBN 979-8-8945-9126-1 (eBook)
Library of Congress Control Number: 2024946242

Printed in Canada/012025/CP20250101

Seahorse Publishing Company
www.seahorsepub.com

Published in the United States
Seahorse Publishing
PO Box 771325
Coral Springs, FL 33077

SEAHORSE PUBLISHING